What the Bible Says About

TONGUES-SPEAKING:

JOHN A. KNIGHT

NAZARENE PUBLISHING HOUSE
Kansas City, Missouri

PRM+
438

Printed in the
United States of America

Cover: Royce Ratcliff

Permission to quote from the following copyrighted versions is acknowl-
edged with appreciation:

The *Modern Language Bible,* the *New Berkeley Version in Modern English*
(NBV), copyright © 1945, 1959, 1969 by Zondervan Publishing House.

The *New American Standard Bible* (NASB), © The Lockman Foundation,
1960, 1962, 1963, 1968, 1971, 1972, 1973, 1975, 1977.

The Holy Bible, New International Version (NIV), copyright © 1973, 1978,
1984 by the International Bible Society.

The *New Testament in Modern English* (Phillips), Revised Edition © J. B. Phillips 1958, 1960, 1972. By permission of the Macmillan Publishing Co.,
Inc.

King James Version (KJV)—Unless otherwise indicated all Scripture quota-
tions are from the KJV.

10 9 8 7 6 5 4 3 2 1

Contents

Introduction   5

Holy Scripture:
  The Primary Basis for Doctrinal
  Affirmation and Practice   11

Manual Declarations:
  The Evidence of the Baptism
  with the Holy Spirit   15

The Nature of the Gift of Tongues   21

Conclusion   33

Notes   37

Addendum   40

Introduction

The practice of tongues-speaking, utterances in an ecstatic or unknown language, is a relatively new phenomenon in the history of Christendom, having its beginnings primarily in the 20th century. This is not to assert that it has never occurred previously either inside or outside the Church. The claim has been made that it was practiced by the Montanists (2nd century), the Irvingites in Britain, and the Mormons in the United States. Mormon choirs used to sing in "tongues." It has been found in non-Christian and pre-Christian or pagan religions before the time of Christ and the New Testament age.

Its beginnings in America can be traced to Charles Parham in Topeka, Kans. (1901). He was the first to claim that tongues-speaking is the evidence of receiving the baptism with the Holy Spirit. Both practice and claim, through the influence of a man named W. J. Seymour, later migrated to the city of Los Angeles, which became the radiating point for its spread across the country. This phenomenon is generally known as the Pentecostal movement, out of which have arisen numerous denominations.

Traditionally its leaders have claimed that speaking in tongues is the evidence of having been filled with, or baptized with, the Holy Spirit. That is, unless one experiences this "glossolalia" or ecstatic utterance one cannot claim to have received the Holy Spirit in fullness. There have been some Pentecostals who have modified this claim slightly to say that tongues-speaking is *an* evidence, that is, one among several evidences. Generally, however, it is viewed as an *indispensable* evidence.

In more recent times, roughly during the past three decades, there has been a marked interest in, and an increased practice of, tongues-speaking. A distinctive element in this "neo-Pentecostal" development has been the fact that it has occurred in many different parts of the world and across a broad spectrum of communions within Christendom—for example, Catholics, Episcopalians, Presbyterians, Congregationalists, Lutherans, Methodists, and so forth. It has been most prominent in churches that have tended to be cold, rationalistic, and liturgical in their worship. The spontaneity, freedom, emotional emphasis, and personal involvement attached to this practice seem to have filled a void or vacuum within many of these worshipers. These old-line churches have become rather lethargic and found a "cure" in the warmth and vitality of this experience and experience-centered worship. The so-called ecumenical (more accurately, independent or anti-institutional) quality, which characterizes some charismatics (tongues-speaking groups or persons), also is appealing to many.

Furthermore, this neo-Pentecostal movement has gained prominence through the televangelists who are known to advocate this practice and in some cases have spoken in tongues or made theological claims regarding it on television. Well-known religious personalities, such as Oral Roberts, Jimmy Swaggart, James Robison, Pat Robertson of The 700 Club, Jim Bakker of PTL notoriety, and others have made the public aware of this practice. Their ministries have prospered, at least in terms of dollars until recently, leading many to conclude that the *practice* of tongues-speaking and its *advocacy* is a key, if not *the* key, to spiritual success (or spirituality). From this it is but a short step to the conclusion that the Holy Spirit is known fully only by persons who engage in tongues-speaking. Other believers too often are viewed, perhaps unconsciously and unintentionally, as second-rate Christians who lack power and the baptism with the Holy Spirit.

This more or less novel development in the Church has met with a wide variety of responses. Some persons have felt that this phenomenon is most assuredly of the Lord and have asserted this position in strong and dogmatic terms. Others have been more cautious, and while not making extreme favorable claims, have been careful not to draw negative conclusions or make rash critical judgments. Large numbers of persons have become confused, not knowing what to believe or how to assess this development. They may even be fearful of concluding or saying something that would blaspheme the Holy Spirit. Others, knowing that this has been found in some pagan religions, have denounced the practice, or even declared that the whole movement—or individual practice—is of the devil. Some, while not going this far, have concluded it is strictly an emotional or subjective experience—

perhaps occasioned in part by deprived or unhealthy emotions.

The position of the Church of the Nazarene regarding the *claim* of the classical Pentecostals that tongues-speaking is *the* evidence or even *an* evidence of the baptism with the Holy Spirit has remained the same throughout her brief history, and it has been clear![1] It has been erroneously assumed by some that the later or newer Pentecostal development, which in part is characterized and popularized by an emphasis on "prayer language," is *basically different* from the earlier or older movement. Consequently, the church's evaluation of the neo-Pentecostal *practice* of a "prayer language" (praying, supposedly in private, in an ecstatic or "unknown" tongue), although stated officially, may not be as well known. Some seem unaware that the church has addressed the issue in an official manner.

This lack of awareness is no doubt also in part because so many new Nazarenes have come into the membership of the church in the last decade or two. Another reason may be that neo-Pentecostals sometimes assert they do not make doctrinal or theological claims regarding the practice, when in fact they often do—implicitly if not explicitly. The assertion is frequently made that this phenomenon is simply that—a practice; and because it is a *religious* practice, it must be acceptable. For some, this tongues-speaking and/or prayer language is a valid experience that has become the norm for evaluating one's own relationship to Christ as well as others' also.

It is this last element—passing spiritual judgment

—that at times produces a condescending attitude toward fellow believers, and evokes criticism, sometimes justified, but at times unduly harsh, of those who practice a prayer language. As a consequence of these and other factors many Christians in the church, believing that the presence of the Spirit should produce unity, are bewildered. Some are becoming disillusioned with ecclesiastical leadership that, in their view, is grieving the Spirit, and not a few have become embittered. Unfortunately, some have been lost to our fellowship.

It seems timely, therefore, that a rationale be given regarding the position of the church on this practice, and that is the aim underlying this brief and incomplete treatise. Other and more fully developed discussions have been published within our ranks[2] as well as without.[3] However, the purpose here is more limited in scope. This is *not a polemic*—not an attempt to *defend* our position as Nazarenes, nor to highlight weaknesses or errors in the views of the Pentecostals or neo-Pentecostals. Rather, the intent is to state the position primarily for the benefit of Nazarenes who desire to be enlightened, and to demonstrate the biblical basis for it.

The church has not taken its stand thoughtlessly, or without reason, as some may have assumed. In our view Scripture does not justify either the *claim* of the Pentecostals or the *practice* (and sometime claims) of the neo-Pentecostals. The method followed is simply to look at the pertinent passages of Scripture and to seek to understand their initial and primary meaning, in an effort to show that the church's teaching on this highly

9

sensitive and sometimes divisive issue arises out of biblical data.

No claim is made to infallibility of understanding or interpretation. Some may disagree either on minor or major points. Hopefully, however, we can demonstrate that the church is not *arbitrary* or *uninformed* in asserting the position she does.

Three main sections will comprise this discussion. First, the criteria for forming doctrinal affirmations and governing practices in the Wesleyan tradition will be noted, although not developed in detail because of space limitations. Second, we will evaluate the *Manual* statement(s) regarding the evidence of the baptism with the Holy Spirit in the light of appropriate scriptures. Third, we will review the position of the church on tongues-speaking and prayer language as stated by the Board of General Superintendents, which is charged by the General Assembly to "be the authority for the interpretation of the law and doctrine of the Church of the Nazarene, and the meaning and force of all provisions of the *Manual,* subject to an appeal to the General Assembly" (*Manual,* par. 318). Specifically, as a means of evaluation we will discuss the nature of the gift of tongues by looking at relevant passages in the Acts of the Apostles and in 1 Corinthians, chapters 12—14. A concluding statement will be made and an appropriate attitude toward tongues-speaking people will be suggested.

Holy Scripture:

The Primary Basis for Doctrinal Affirmation and Practice

Dr. H. Orton Wiley, dean of Nazarene theologians, said: "Holy Scripture is recognized by all schools as the true source of Christian theology."[4] Theological affirmations are to be judged primarily by their adherence to the clear teachings of the Bible. Other criteria such as tradition (community experience), reason (the canons of logic), or experience (personal religious experience) may have limited validity, but any doctrinal view contrary to the Scriptures must be rejected. Historically Christian theology has given mediate authority to one or another of these secondary sources.[5]

We in the Wesleyan tradition have always maintained that these secondary criteria are at best only confirmatory. They are insufficient in and of themselves to establish doctrine. Furthermore, they have obvious weaknesses. For example, religious experience, which is frequently exalted by and appears to be primary data for most who espouse tongues-speaking, is fraught with dangers apart from the correction and evaluation of Scripture. Dr. Richard S. Taylor, respected Wesleyan scholar, has commented on this point with great clarity:

When men experience God, they possess immediate certainty which becomes for them a touchstone of truth. Every theory tends to be evaluated by that experience. But since men and women are not only sinful but very complex and elusive in their susceptibility to delusion and suggestion, it is inevitable that religious experience may mislead as well as guide. The possible variations in religious experience seem endless, and as a consequence experience is a shaky ground for the development of a theological system. By itself experience has no safeguards against the extremes and vagaries of mystical, irrational subjectivism. The "God" men experience may not be the God and Father of our Lord Jesus Christ.[6]

Tradition, which is technically *expanded* personal religious experience, or group experience, may be more reliable but remains inadequate. Taylor continues:

The broader wisdom of the community, rooted in its own tradition and history, provides a check on the individual. Private experience needs to be subject to the judgment of others, especially those older and more mature.

But the community itself may be in error, and the error may only reproduce itself in repeated private experiences. The psychology of religious experience is such that what the group expects is often what the person seeks—and even obtains. The phenomenon of tongues, for instance, almost never occurs spontaneously without prior or concurrent group pressure, even though overt influence may have occurred in the past and be buried in the subconscious. We must confess therefore that even the combination of experience and community is not adequate for a sound theology. Experience may be false, or at least misinterpreted, while the community may be perpetuating a distortion, if not a heresy.[7]

The point being made may refer to any group or branch of Christendom that exalts experience or tradition to a place of supremacy. It is for this reason that Nazarenes insist that the Bible be accepted as "the authorizing source and norm for theological thought and action."[8]

Obviously the Scriptures must be interpreted. Outlining and establishing the principles of biblical interpretation (hermeneutics) cannot be done here. Suffice it to say that all interpretation is to be done in the light of the highest and best we know, namely, the revelation in Jesus Christ. The Scriptures are to be understood by Him, as He and the Scriptures are made known by the Holy Spirit. Thus our view of Scripture is not cold, rationalistic, legalistic, or dogmatic. We believe the Spirit illuminates the mind, and we accept whatever legitimate scholarly tools are available to arrive at the soundest and most reliable view of any given passage of Scripture.

When Nazarenes affirm loyalty to the Word of God, they are saying the Scriptures are the primary source of spiritual knowledge and insight. Doctrinal affirmations and normative practice are not to arise out of sociological trends (not even those inside the community of believers), or the latest psychological theories, or the result of some Gallup poll, or any esoteric or private experience of an alleged encounter with

13

God. Rather, they are born of and are informed and judged by the teachings of Scripture.

Where there are those who differ with us or our interpretations, we do not unchristianize them nor assess their spirituality in a judgmental manner. The *Manual* of the church states that we require of church members doctrinally "only such avowals of belief as are essential to Christian experience"—that is, are clearly required in the Scriptures for salvation. Further, the *Manual* declares "that the Old and New Testament Scriptures, given by plenary inspiration, contain all truth necessary to faith and Christian living" (par. 25.2). Therefore, the Scriptures alone are our guide for salvation and effective Christian witness.

In matters nonessential to salvation, we permit liberty. With regard to those that in our view are essential to salvation, we require adherence to our doctrinal affirmations of all who would become a part of our fellowship as Nazarenes. And, in addition, we refuse to make any doctrinal claim without solid biblical foundation, or to permit any practice in our congregations where there is obvious biblical reservation.[9]

Manual Declarations:

The Evidence of the Baptism with the Holy Spirit

In the light of the claim of classical Pentecostals and some neo-Pentecostals that evidence of the baptism with the Holy Spirit is speaking in tongues, the position of the Church of the Nazarene should be known. It is stated in two places in the *Manual*. The first is in the Church Constitution, Articles of Faith, X (par. 13). The article is titled "Entire Sanctification" by which "believers are made free from original sin, or depravity, and brought into a state of entire devotement to God, and the holy obedience of love made perfect." This relationship with God in Christ is "known by various terms representing its different phases, such as . . . 'the baptism with the Holy Spirit' . . ."

The *evidences* of this divine work are stated thus: "It [entire sanctification] is wrought by the baptism with the Holy Spirit, and comprehends in one experience [subsequent to regeneration] the cleansing of the heart from sin and the abiding, indwelling presence of the Holy Spirit, empowering the believer for life and service."

The evidences given are *purity* (heart cleansing), *power* (for service and victorious living), and *the witness of the Spirit*.

The second reference in the *Manual* is found in the Appendix (par. 905), under the heading "Evidence of Baptism with the Holy Spirit." It reads:

> We believe that the Holy Spirit bears witness to the new birth and to the subsequent work of heart cleansing, or entire sanctification, through the infilling of the Holy Spirit.
>
> We affirm that the one biblical evidence of entire sanctification, or the infilling of the Holy Spirit [that is, the *indispensable* evidence that as the paragraph proceeds to say may take a variety of forms] is the cleansing of the heart by faith from original sin as stated in Acts 15:8-9: "And God, which knoweth the hearts, bare them witness, giving them the Holy Ghost, even as he did unto us: and put no difference between us and them, purifying their hearts by faith." And this cleansing is manifested by the fruit of the Spirit in a holy life. "But the fruit of the Spirit is love, joy, peace, long-suffering, gentleness, goodness, faith, meekness, temperance: against such there is no law. And they that are Christ's have crucified the flesh with the affections and lusts" [Galatians 5:22-24].
>
> To affirm that even a special or any alleged physical evidence, or "prayer language," is evidence of the baptism with the Spirit is contrary to the biblical and historic position of the church. [1985]

This reference, like the first one, speaks of *heart purity, power* to manifest the fruit of the Spirit (which manifestations are the virtues of Christ), and of the *witness of the Spirit.* Specifically, it denies tongues-speaking, including "prayer language," as being *the* evidence, or even *an* evidence, of being filled with the Holy Spirit.

Since the Scriptures, and not experience or other data, must determine our doctrinal positions, we must ask, "What does the Bible say regarding the evidence(s) of baptism with the Holy Spirit?"

It says that *we can know or be assured of our relationship with God* and also *how we can know.*[10] We Wesleyans refer to this knowledge as "the witness of the Spirit" or "Christian assurance." (This along with the possibility of entire sanctification are *the* two distinctive elements of our *theology,* and should be of our *preaching* and *teaching.*)

1. Six times John says in his First Epistle that we know (we are assured that we are in harmony with God because of certain factors):

3:14—we know because we "love the brethren"

2:3—we know because we "keep his commandments"

2:5—we know the love of God is "perfected" in us because we keep His Word

4:16-19—we know because we have "boldness" (feel comfortable or assured) for the day of judgment

3:24—we know "by the Spirit which he hath given us"

2:29—we know we are born of God because we "do" righteousness (live a Christlike and ethical life)

Summary: John, the apostle whom Jesus loved, was inspired by God and is a credible witness. He saw

Christ before and after His death; he saw the empty tomb; he saw Jesus ascend to heaven; he was at Pentecost and spoke in languages; he healed and preached in power. But he relied on none of these things. He gave as his evidence of being right with God the *power* to love, obey Christ's commandments, and live righteously, or as the *Manual* states it: "The holy obedience of love made perfect" (par. 13).

* * *

2. Like John, Peter also says we can know. He states that we have been "begotten . . . unto a lively hope" (1 Pet. 1:3), and that we have the witness of the Spirit. Speaking of the coming of the Holy Spirit upon the house of Cornelius he said, after years of reflection on its significance, the Spirit "bare them witness . . . *purifying* their hearts by faith" (Acts 15:8-9, italic added).

Summary: Peter in many ways was the staunchest of the apostles. His testimony also is reliable. He did everything John did. In addition, he introduced the new age to Jews and Gentiles; he raised the dead, healed, and preached in power. But he gave none of these things as evidences of being filled with the Spirit. Rather, he declared *heart purity* as the evidence.

* * *

3. Likewise the apostle Paul affirmed that we can know or be assured of the presence of the Spirit in our lives:

1 Thess. 1:5—he rejoices in "much assurance"

Eph. 4:30 and 2 Cor. 1:21-22—he says that God

18

has "sealed us, and given the earnest of the Spirit in our hearts" (2 Cor. 1:22) "unto the day of redemption" (Eph. 4:30)

Gal. 4:6—we know because God has sent His Spirit into our hearts, crying, "Abba, Father"

Summary: Paul laid the foundation of the Church among the Gentiles; he saw the resurrected Christ (Christ "appeared" to him [Acts 26:16]); he received revelations from God; he was caught up into heaven; he saw visions of God; he healed the sick, cast out devils, and raised the dead. But he pointed to none of these things as evidence of the fullness of the Spirit. Rather, he appealed to the *personal witness of the personal Holy Spirit with his spirit.*

* * *

These biblical giants and divinely inspired writers give the evidence(s) of the baptism with the Spirit. They are:

- PERFECT LOVE (holy boldness or power for Christlike living)
- HEART PURITY (cleansing of inward, as well as outward, sin)
- THE WITNESS OF THE SPIRIT (including the fruit of the Spirit)

These evidences in this age of the Spirit remain until this day.

John Wesley helped us put this witness, or evidence, or assurance, or confirmation in perspective. He said we know we are accepted of God and have received His Spirit by the *witness* of the Spirit and by the *fruit* of the Spirit. The witness of the Spirit is noted by:

1. the objective witness—this is God's Word and promise (e.g., Ezek. 36:25-27; 1 John 1:7, 9)

2. the subjective witness—this includes the "direct" witness of God's Spirit with our spirit. There is "no condemnation" and we feel comfortable in (enjoy) His presence. Accompanying this direct witness is the indirect witness, which is the fruit (singular) of the Spirit in our lives (Gal. 5:22-23):

- love, joy, peace (inner life of the believer)
- long-suffering, kindness, goodness (these relate to personal relationships and suffering)
- faithfulness, meekness, self-control (demonstrated in individual and ordinary circumstances of life)

This fruit is the spiritual harvest within the life of the believer. It is not a "work"; it is the Holy Spirit's doing. Fruit comes from "walking in the Spirit" (Gal. 5:16, 25) and "sowing" to the Spirit (6:7-8).

When Christians stop sowing they become ineffective and powerless. But this fruit can and should increase and grow, or abound (2 Pet. 1:5-8; also 1 Thess. 3:12; 4:10). We acknowledge and insist on the difference between *purity* and *maturity* (2 Cor. 3:18; *Manual,* par. 14).

The Nature of the Gift of Tongues

We have attempted to show on the basis of Scripture the marks of being filled with the Spirit. In general terms, we may say that evidence of being indwelt or baptized with the Spirit is the fruit of the Spirit, and not the gifts of the Spirit.

This is not to deny the gifts or that they are present in the church in the 20th century. "From the beginning we have believed that the authentic gifts of the Spirit belong to the Church. While it is God's will that every believer should be baptized and empowered with the Holy Spirit, it is not God's promise that every believer should receive any particular gift [see 1 Cor. 12:8-10, 28-30]. On the contrary, the gifts are distributed by the Holy Spirit to the various believers according to the Spirit's sovereign will (1 Corinthians 12:11)." (See also Eph. 4:7; Heb. 2:4.)[11]

The gifts of the Spirit are named in four different passages in the New Testament: Rom. 12:6-8; 1 Cor. 12:4-11, 28-30; Eph. 4:7-8, 11-13;[12] and 1 Pet. 4:9-11. They are listed at times by *function* and at times by *person* or *role*. Twenty or 21 gifts are mentioned, depending on whether the work of pastor is separated from that of a teacher in Eph. 4:11. Without giving the

21

content of each, we list them as follows: prophecy ("forth-telling"), teaching, apostles, healings, interpretation (translation) of languages, kinds of languages (gift of plural languages unlearned by the person speaking, and given in an evangelistic context), miraculous powers, serving (*diakonia*, from which we get our words *deacon* and *deaconess*), gifts of administration, discerning of spirits, encouraging, (evangelists), faith, giving, helps (assisting financially), knowledge, leadership (ability to lead as a shepherd gives care to his flock), showing mercy (compassion), pastors, speaking (words prompted by the Holy Spirit), and wisdom.

Scripture makes several facts clear regarding the gifts.

a. Each believer has at least one gift (1 Cor. 7:7).

b. The gift is to be used for God's glory.

c. Gifts are for the edification of the church or for evangelism (1 Cor. 12:7), and not for the aggrandizement or titillation of one's own self (Eph. 4:7-12).

d. The Spirit not only distributes the gifts but also controls the gifts. Thus a gift can be withdrawn or given repeatedly.

e. We are not enjoined to pray for a specific gift, except for the gift of interpretation (translation) if one is given the gift of languages (1 Cor. 14:13). However, it is not necessarily wrong to pray for a gift. But a gift other than that of languages is to be preferred (12:31; 14:1, 12, 19, 39).

f. Gifts are not proof, or evidence, of *spirituality*.

Corinth, which seems to have been preoccupied with the gifts, was Paul's biggest problem church.

g. Prophecy, which is preaching or proclamation of the Word, is to be emphasized most and languages least (1 Cor. 14:1-5, 23-25, 39).

h. Authentic gifts of the Spirit are not "earned" and they are not "learned." One can teach psychological manifestations but not gifts of the Spirit.

i. One can choose *not* to use one's gift (1 Cor. 14:32). This is to "grieve the Spirit" (Eph. 4:30). But one cannot use or manifest a gift anytime one chooses.

Since we do not deny that the gifts of the Spirit are operable in the Church today as the Spirit desires, then we must ask, "What is the nature of the particular gift in question, namely, the gift of tongues or languages?" The Scripture alone must be the source of our answer, so we must look at those passages in the New Testament that allude to tongues-speaking.

We have noted earlier that "unknown" or ecstatic tongues is found in some non-Christian and pagan cults; it is also practiced in some forms of *exorcism*. Further, we have asserted that whatever this gift is, it is not an evidence of being filled with the Holy Spirit (although every classic Pentecostal leader says that it is such). Rather, it is a "sign" for unbelievers, not believers (1 Cor. 14:22).

What, then, is the "tongues" spoken of in the Scriptures?

An official statement of the church[13] replies thus:

> The gift of tongues is related to the miraculous gift of many languages on the Day of Pentecost. On that great day the Church was enabled to cross language barriers. The people present were astonished because each one heard the gospel being preached in his own native dialect (Acts 2:6, 8). This special miracle was an expression of God's desire to reach every man everywhere through the spoken and written word. Language is the vehicle of God's truth.
>
> We believe that the biblical material supports one authentic gift—a language given to communicate the gospel and not an unknown babble of sounds . . .

Does the Scripture provide a rationale for this stance that tongues is the gift of plural languages? We believe it does.

Gerrit Verkuyl in the Berkeley version translates "kinds of tongues" (KJV, 1 Cor. 12:10) as "unfamiliar languages." Tongues is not ecstatic utterance. The Greek word *ektasis* is never used to refer to speaking in tongues or to the speaker in tongues. Tongues is not "unknown" in the Pentecostal or neo-Pentecostal sense. (The word *unknown* is in italics in KJV to indicate this is not in the New Testament manuscripts.) The word translated "tongues" (*glossa*) means "language" or "dialect" (*dialekto*, Acts 2:6, 8) spoken by a people. *Glossa,* and not *ektasis* (ecstasy), is used all through the New Testament, including Corinthians, to mean "languages."

In seeking to answer the question as to the nature

24

of tongues, it is imperative to observe the passages where tongues are referred to in the Scripture:

    a. Acts 2—first Christian Pentecost (*a known language*—each person heard "in his own native language," v. 8, NIV)

    b. Acts 10—Caesarea (house of Cornelius)

    c. Acts 19—Ephesian disciples

Luke, who records these events, does not distinguish Acts 10 and 19 from Acts 2. The cultural and linguistic backgrounds were similar, and in each case there were persons of different nationalities and linguistic backgrounds present. We know the tongues in Acts 2 were known languages (dialects), and there is no reason to assume it was different on the other occasions (see Acts 10:46 and 19:6). In all three cases the *gift of an unlearned language* was given for purposes of evangelization at significant times in the advance of the gospel. We are being taught that the gospel is universal and *for all classes:*

    Acts 2—for the birthright Jews, including those dispersed all over the Mediterranean world

    Acts 10—for proselyte Jews (Gentiles converted to Judaism)

    Acts 19—for Gentiles (non-Jews) with no connection with Judaism

By anybody's chronology the Acts of the Apostles was written at least six years, perhaps as much as nine years, after 1 Corinthians. If ecstatic or "unknown" utterances were important, surely Luke, Paul's longtime companion, would have said so. It was most likely Luke, who was sent by the apostle to Corinth (2 Cor.

8:18), giving the "beloved physician" and author of Acts firsthand knowledge of the situation described in 1 Corinthians 14.

* * *

NOTE: It is instructive to observe that the Gospels do not mention "unknown tongues." Mark 16:17, which speaks of "new tongues" [*glossais . . . kainais*—even here the reference is not to "ecstatic" tongues] is not in the best and earliest manuscripts, and most authorities agree is a redaction. The entire package includes "taking up serpents" (v. 18). Further, Jesus never spoke in "tongues" or encouraged His disciples to do so, even when they asked Him, "Lord, teach us to pray" (Luke 11:1).

* * *

d. 1 Corinthians 12—14—Corinth

Nowhere else in Scripture, aside from these four passages, is there a reference to tongues. It is significant that the issue came up in a church beset with quarreling, lawsuits among the members, sexual immorality (even incest), drunkenness at the Lord's Supper, confusion in the public services—which may have included some kind of incomprehensible utterances (this is implied in 14:2 though by no means certain), and even curses against Christ (12:3).

Much of this can be attributed to the cultural and religious backgrounds of the people, many of whom had been converted recently out of paganism.

In 1 Cor. 12:1 Paul says he does not want the Corinthians "ignorant" of spiritual matters (not spiritual

26

gifts as in some translations since one word is used, *pneumatikon*). They had wrongly assumed that gifts were a sign of being "spiritual." (Apparently they had written to Paul asking about mixed marriages, offering meat to idols, etc.) The congregation had "enthusiasm" but was "ignorant" (uninformed or uninstructed, immature). They gave their peak emotional experiences absolute status. Experience became the highest category in their theology, rather than ethics and the fruit of the Spirit. The Corinthians were interested in the mystical or "exalted" (not the "earthly") Jesus; in His heavenly power, and not His earthly *mission.* So unbalanced were they that at least some among them were saying, Let the "earthbound" Jesus be "accursed" *(anathema)* (12:3).

Paul's response is immediate and penetrating. His pneumatology or his teaching on the Holy Spirit is Christ-centered, and his primary interest is to promote Christlikeness in the believer. Thus, he says, the Holy Spirit is not a free-lancer. He is the Spirit of Jesus. To underscore the meaning of spirituality, he asks: Does your experience testify to the Spirit operative in that earthly Jesus—compassion for neighbor, the downtrodden, the dispossessed? Or are you more concerned about your own feelings, your variable subjective emotions, your spiritual pulse, than about your responsibility?

Christ came in the flesh—to say otherwise is the spirit of antichrist. Jesus is the Norm, the content of the Spirit. Thus the Father is a Christlike God, and the Holy Spirit is a Christlike Spirit. So in these three chap-

27

ters (12, 13, 14) Paul gives the marks (the Spirit) of Jesus:

1 Corinthians 12—grace to *serve* others (*charismata*, gracious powers, outgoing mercy)

1 Corinthians 13—strength to *love* others ("charity," *charis*, more than mere vague feeling but the active seeking of the well-being of others, even one's enemies)

1 Corinthians 14—power to *build up* others; to *communicate;* to tear down walls; to avoid talking "churchese" so as to talk to those outside the church

Let's review key ideas and verses in these chapters.

1 Corinthians 12. The gifts listed in this chapter (vv. 8-10, 28-30) are "grace gifts." They are not the ability to do something miraculous necessarily, but they infuse one's life with the power of God's Spirit. These gifts are for the communication of the gospel—"for the perfecting [equipping] of the saints, for the work of ministry" (Eph. 4:12-13).

There are no "unknown" tongues listed here. The gift of tongues (languages) in verse 10 is the God-given ability to speak different (real) languages in a multilingual city for the spreading of the gospel. In chapter 14 Paul gives a fundamental principle and one of his primary emphases: If a language is to have value, it must communicate. Otherwise it is not to be used. Speaking in languages is to assist in certain times of evangelism, to build up the church through communication.

NOTE: This principle of communication seems to rule out prayer language, which is based more on a person's experience than on the Word of God. See Addendum.

* * *

1 Corinthians 13. Here love *(agape)*, God's kind of love, is shown to be superior to every gift: "Covet earnestly the best gifts: and yet shew I unto you a more excellent way" (12:31).

Some have assumed that "tongues of angels" (v. 1) refers to unknown or ecstatic tongues. But the phrase is used in a hypothetical sense: even *if* one could speak as an angel, it is of no value without love. Paul never suggested anyone could speak like an angel, certainly not the Corinthian Christians.

1 Corinthians 14. Paul uses the word *pneumatika* (spirituality) rather than *charismata* (gifts) and does not refer to the Holy Spirit in this chapter. Only here (v. 2), for the first time, does he speak of a language that is not understood. But he does not call it a gift. There may have been unknown utterances practiced in Corinth since some had been converted out of pagan religions where this was practiced. However, this is only an inference and is not explicitly expressed.[14]

Paul is talking about the authentic gift of languages. This is clear from the fact that the "tongue" (language) can be "interpreted" (translated). Only bonafide languages can be translated.

Further, Paul says in 14:4 that a speaker of a language that others do not understand only edifies the speaker. If the speaker himself does not understand it, then Paul is contradictory, for such a person could not be edified since communication is necessarily involved. *Communication* is the key.

In verse 5 Paul says he wishes all spoke in *tongues* (languages). He certainly doesn't mean tongues that "curse" Christ (12:3), or that could not be understood by others, nor even not understood by oneself. He says they ought to pray for the ability to *interpret* (translate). He is not referring to an unknown or ecstatic utterance. Paul observes that he speaks (in number) "more [languages] than you all" (v. 18, NASB). The Corinthians were spiritually proud, so he mildly boasts a little himself. He spoke Hebrew, Greek, Latin, and probably Aramaic. He says he would rather speak five words intelligently in one of these languages than "10,000 words" that were not understood (v. 19).

Verses 14-19 have been interpreted to imply meaningless utterance, or to support "prayer language." Verse 14 says, "My understanding is unfruitful," which is erroneously understood as "uncomprehending." However, this does not mean the mind is uninvolved or does not understand. Rather, the Greek *(akarpos)* says the mind is "unproductive"—that is, does not communicate on an intellectual level. In other words, "If I pray in another language, others may sense my spirit, but what I am saying is not fruitful for them since they cannot understand."

Verses 21-22 have been widely misunderstood. They are from Isa. 28:11-13, spoken when the prophet had been scorned by priests and leaders who were "confused with wine" (NASB) and staggered under "strong drink" (NASB). Drunk, they rejected God's words through His true prophet, who said the next time God would speak would be through an enemy with a strange or foreign language (Assyrian), not only in words but also in deeds.

Thus in these verses Paul is saying that "tongues" (either languages untranslated for uncomprehending hearers or unintelligible utterances) were evidence of confusion; and any unbeliever who heard would say the speakers were "mad"—crazy (v. 23). This confusion will incur God's judgment, or perhaps, is even a sign of God's judgment.

* * *

OBSERVATION: The proliferation of languages at the Tower of Babel was the result of the judgment of God on the pride of men. The demonstration at Pentecost where every man heard the gospel in his own language or dialect was the reversal, the opposite of God's judgment.

* * *

The proponents of tongues-speaking frequently appeal to verse 39: "Wherefore, brethren, covet to prophesy, and forbid not to speak with tongues." This seems to be contrary to what has been spoken earlier. In fact Paul *does* forbid speaking in tongues (unfamiliar languages) when certain conditions obtain: *(a)* two or at the most three persons have already spoken (v. 27); *(b)* there is no translator (v. 28)—in Corinth, a multilingual city, it was not always easy to know if a strange speech were a true language; and further the purpose of speech is communication; *(c)* when the person desiring to speak is a woman (v. 34).

This context strongly suggests that the translation of verse 39 is in error. Not only is it inconsistent with the rest of the chapter, but further no one in Corinth desired to forbid speaking unfamiliar languages. The word translated "forbid not" *(me koluete)* can mean "hinder" (see Acts 11:17) and may be rendered "impede not." Further, it is quite possible that *tolalein* ("to speak") refers not to tongues (languages) but to prophesying. Therefore, we may translate the verse the opposite of what appears in the KJV: "Strongly desire to prophesy [preach] and do not hinder your proclamation by unknown [or unintelligible] tongues [languages]." The Greek may bear this rendering, and further, it brings inner consistency to all Paul has been saying.[15]

In handling the confusing situation at Corinth Paul insisted that all regulations (vv. 27-35) be followed: "Let all things be done decently and in order" (v. 40).

Conclusion

There is a true *charisma* (gift) of tongues (languages). It is the gift of speaking another language unlearned by the speaker. This gift, like the other authentic gifts, is of the Spirit. There is no *charisma* of an unknown tongue or ecstatic utterance given by the Spirit, or at least no sufficient biblical evidence to conclude that there is such.

An "unknown" tongue does not meet the biblical criterion of usefulness *(communication)*; it lacks biblical basis; it calls attention to itself and away from inward and outward holiness. It is not "rational"—thus Phillips paraphrases 14:20, "Don't be children, but use your intelligence!"

Glossolalia (unknown utterance), if not a psychological phenomenon as some authorities claim, is a subjective and esoteric, experience-oriented practice. The Holy Spirit may be present where it exists; people may even be converted. But this is not an endorsement.

As a consequence of this perspective, an official statement was published in the *Herald of Holiness* October 15, 1976, over the signatures of members of the Board of General Superintendents, under the title "The Position of the Church of the Nazarene on Speaking in Tongues." Careful elaboration was given, but the essence of the proclamation is as follows:

. . . any practice and/or propagation of speaking in tongues either as the evidence of the baptism with the Holy Spirit or as a neo-pentecostal ecstatic prayer language shall be interpreted as inveighing against the doctrines and usages of the Church of the Nazarene.[16]

It should be apparent from our study that the Church of the Nazarene is not arbitrary in the position it takes regarding tongues-speaking, either in public or as a prayer language. There is a rationale with a biblical foundation for our historic stance.

What should be our attitude toward tongues-speaking persons?

1. Love them.
2. Do not practice this, nor permit its practice in our circles, but stick to our mission of preaching, teaching, and promoting scripturally based heart holiness. Where Christ sanctifies *wholly* He satisfies fully.
3. Emphasize the normal pattern of Christian living in 1 Corinthians 13 and Romans 8 and 12.

This attitude, which is consonant with the Spirit of Christ, is clearly advanced in "The Position of the Church of the Nazarene on Speaking in Tongues":

In taking this stand, we do not wish to reflect on the sincerity or integrity of those who differ with us on these matters. We recognize as fellow members of His universal body all who are in Christ and extend to them the right hand of Christian fellowship. However, our direction as a church is clear, and we desire this direction and stand to be understood by all.

We believe that good stewardship would dictate that we unitedly expend our energies within the framework of those biblical doctrines and practices to which we are firmly committed. Only by so doing can we most effectively advance the kingdom of God and fulfill our mandate to spread scriptural holiness to the ends of the earth.

Notes

1. In 1919 the word *Pentecostal* was deleted from the name "Pentecostal Church of the Nazarene," since the youthful denomination had never aligned itself with the Pentecostal movement and wished to dissociate itself from it in the minds of the populace.

2. Harvey J. S. Blaney, *Speaking in Unknown Tongues: The Pauline Position* (Kansas City: Beacon Hill Press of Kansas City, 1973).

Charles D. Isbell, "Glossolalia and Propheteialalia: A Study of 1 Corinthians 14," *Wesleyan Theological Journal* 10 (Spring 1975).

Donald S. Metz, *Speaking in Tongues* (Kansas City: Nazarene Publishing House, 1964).

Norman R. Oke, *Facing the Tongues Issue* (Kansas City: Beacon Hill Press of Kansas City, 1973).

W. T. Purkiser, *Spiritual Gifts: Healing and Tongues—The Charismatic Revival* (Kansas City: Nazarene Publishing House, 1964).

W. T. Purkiser, *The Gifts of the Spirit* (Kansas City: Beacon Hill Press of Kansas City, 1975).

Timothy L. Smith, *Speaking the Truth in Love: Some Honest Questions for Pentecostals* (Kansas City: Beacon Hill Press of Kansas City, 1977). (Originally presented at the annual meeting of the Society for Pentecostal Study, Ann Arbor, Mich.: December 3, 1975.)

Richard S. Taylor, *Tongues: Their Purpose and Meaning* (Kansas City: Beacon Hill Press of Kansas City, 1973).

3. Wesley L. Duewel, *The Holy Spirit and Tongues* (Winona Lake, Ind.: Light and Life Press, 1974).

Lloyd H. Knox, *Key Biblical Perspectives on Tongues* (Winona Lake, Ind.: Light and Life Press, 1974).

John J. Robertson, *Tongues: What You Should Know About Glossolalia* (Mountain View, Calif.: Pacific Press Publishing Association, 1977).

4. H. Orton Wiley, *Christian Theology* (Kansas City: Beacon Hill Press, 1940), 1:167.

5. Robert K. Johnston in a review of *Authority and the Renewal of American Theology,* by Dennis M. Campbell (Philadelphia: United Church Press, 1976), in *Christianity Today,* November 18, 1977.

6. Richard S. Taylor, *Biblical Authority and Christian Faith* (Kansas City: Beacon Hill Press of Kansas City, 1980), 23-24.

7. Ibid., 25-26.

8. Frederick Herzog as quoted by Campbell and cited ibid., 28.

9. *Observation:* Although not specifically germane to our topic, it may be noted that the Nazarene tradition, like most traditions, is unwritten and broader than mere doctrinal "orthodoxy." It encompasses such things as *style* of worship, including music and freedom of expression. There is much diversity among us, but certain parameters are sensed and recognized. Nazarenes, for example, normally do not claim categorically that God told them to do a certain thing, such as to deliver or convey a specific message to another person, etc. They believe in and accept God's leadership, but the articulation of it is couched in more reticent language. Acts 15:28 illustrates this reticence: "So it *seemed* good to the Holy Ghost, and to us . . ." To be more direct, or to attribute more to God than this inner conviction, would appear to presume on the Divine.

In the second century the Montanists, who emphasized the Holy Spirit to the virtual exclusion of every other Christian tenet, were declared heretics by the church, not primarily because of what they taught, but because of their mood and spirit. They were not unorthodox doctrinally; but they were dogmatic, harsh, and abrasive, and also given to emotionalism, sentimentality, and "faddish practices." Divisiveness and spiritual elitism often were their environment. Their emphases became imbalanced. There is a proper *mood and spirit,* as well as *correct teaching,* in our Nazarene heritage. To state it differently, our heritage has a *doctrinal content* that can be *taught;* it also has a *perspective,* a *spirit* that can only be *caught.* And that spirit must be judged and nurtured by 1 Corinthians 13, which describes the "more excellent way" of divine love.

10. On this point I have been instructed by a former college professor, now deceased, Dr. W. N. King, of Bethany Nazarene College.

11. Board of General Superintendents' Statement, *Herald of Holiness,* October 15, 1976.

12. It is questionable as to whether these verses in Ephesians should be included in the list of gifts since *charismata* (special gifts such as those noted in 1 Cor. 12:4-11) is not used. The Greek term *domata* (a general term for that which is given) is used instead. These gifts are the gifted men—apostles, evangelists, pastors—mentioned in 4:11.

13. See reference in n. 11.

14. While some authorities claim that ecstatic utterance was the Corinthian practice, there is no conclusive evidence to support the claim. It can only be arrived at by an inference drawn primarily from 14:2. Even if the claim were correct, it is not asserted in Scripture that ecstatic utterance is the authentic gift of tongues or languages.

15. See Purkiser, *Gifts of the Spirit,* 67; also Charles D. Isbell, "Glossolalia and Propheteialalia," 18-20.

16. See *Manual* paragraph 26.3, from the General Rules, which enjoins Nazarenes to "evidence their commitment to God" and the church "by abiding in hearty fellowship with the church, not inveighing against but wholly committed to its doctrines and usages . . ."

Addendum

Wesley L. Duewel in *The Holy Spirit and Tongues* (pp. 49-50) asks the following questions for "Prayer Language Advocates":

1. We are to love the Lord with our *mind*—why "bypass" it?
2. How can God reserve this for a select few if it is necessary for the Christian's walk?
3. If tongues is the least gift, how is it a better form of prayer?
4. If it edifies, why pray for the gift of interpretation (14:13)?
5. Why didn't Jesus thus teach His disciples?
6. Why is it not taught *clearly* in Scripture?
7. We are to discern the spirits—how can one in *private* be sure of the Spirit?
8. If the mind is "unfruitful," how can one be sure what he prays or when prayer is answered?
9. How can faith be exercised if we don't know for what we are praying?